Written and illustrated
by David Kennett

SOLOS

For Lizzie

Southwood Books Limited
3-5 Islington High St
London N1 9LQ

First published in Australia by Omnibus Books 2002
This edition published in the UK under licence from
Omnibus Books by
Southwood Books Limited 2002

Cover design by Lyn Mitchell
Typeset by Clinton Ellicott, Adelaide
Printed in Singapore

ISBN 1 903207 66 5

A CIP catalogue record for this book is available
from the British Library.

The chimpanzee

- is a warm-blooded animal
- is the mammal most like a human
- can learn to communicate with humans
- uses sticks or branches as weapons
- is one of the noisiest wild animals – its call can be heard kilometres away.

There are not as many chimpanzees living today as there have been in the past.

Chimpanzees are forest animals. As the forests are cut down there are fewer places for chimpanzees to live.

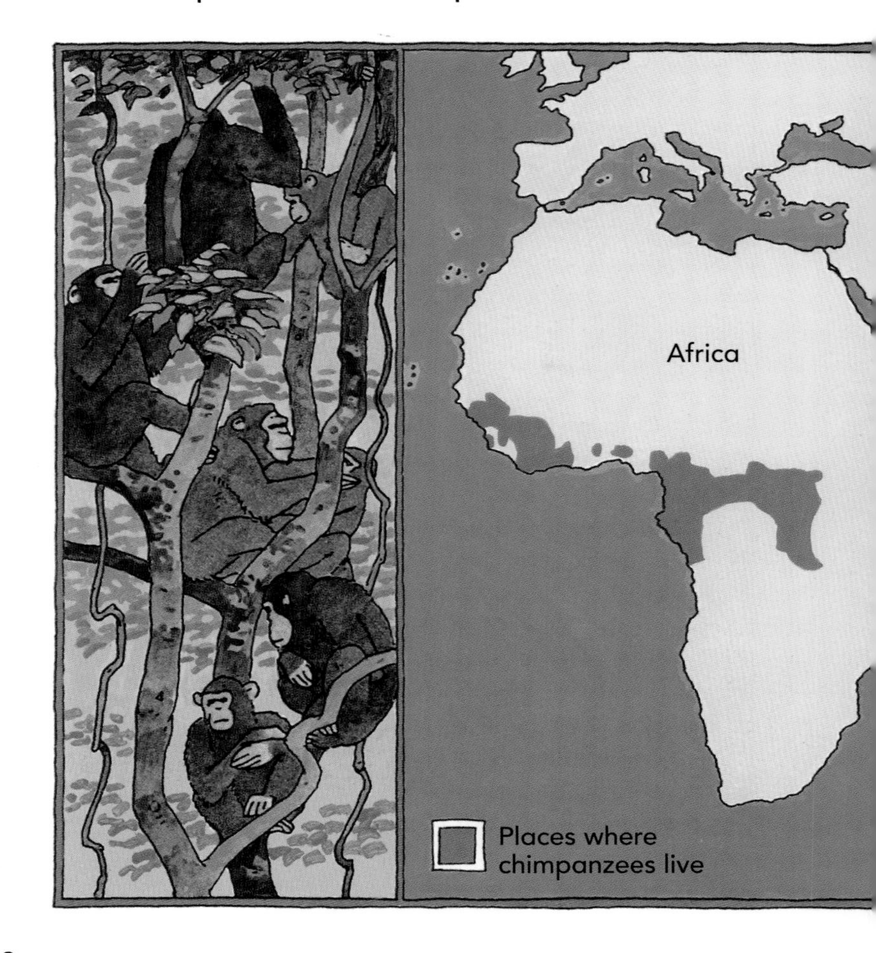

In Africa there are still some forests and national parks where chimpanzees live in the wild.

This map shows where chimpanzees live now.

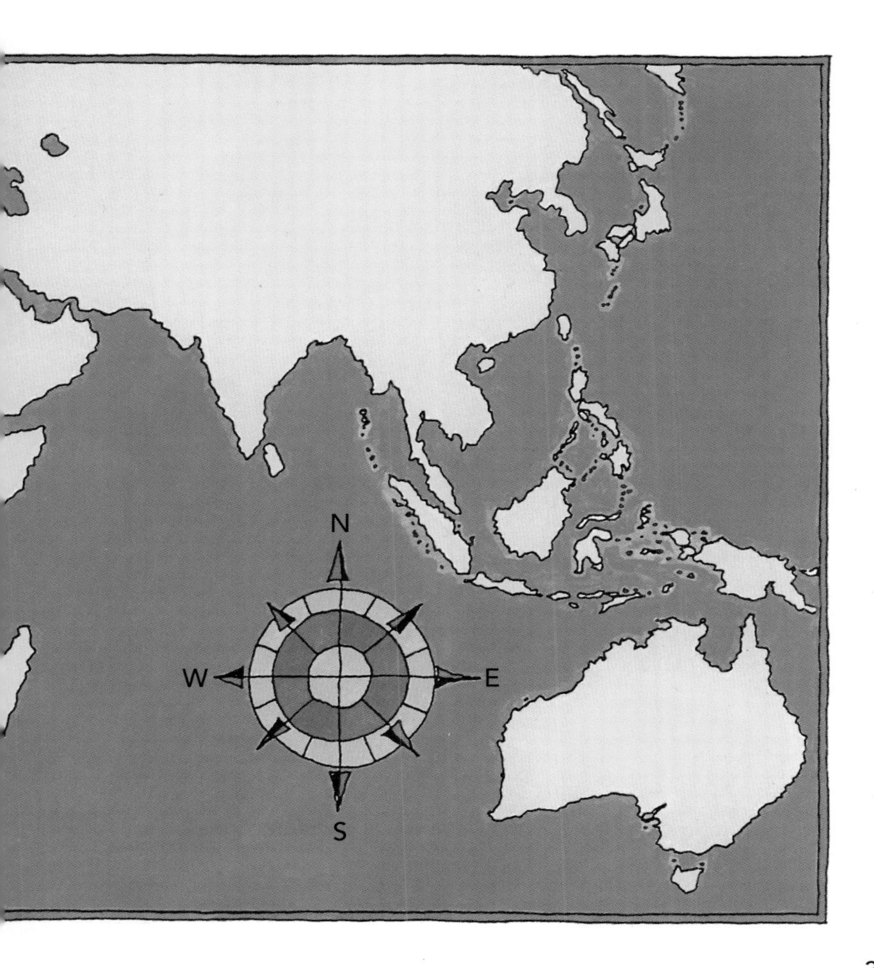

The chimpanzee is one of a group of animals called the primates. There are about 230 primates, including humans.

Here are some primates. The maps show where each one lives.

Vervet
monkey
Ring-
tailed
lemur
Gorilla
De Brazza guenon
Baboon
120
140
160
180
200 centimetres

Male chimpanzees can be bigger than females. This male chimpanzee measures 90 centimetres from his rump to his nose. He is 78 centimetres tall, measured from the top of his shoulder to the ground.

90 centimetres
78 centimetres

This male chimpanzee weighs
49 kilograms. A house cat weighs
about three and a half kilograms.
You would need 14 cats to make up
the same weight as this chimpanzee.

Male chimpanzees are heavier than females. Female chimpanzees weigh about 30 kilograms.

This male
chimpanzee is
137 centimetres tall
when he is standing
on two legs.

Most of the time
chimpanzees walk
with their hands
and feet on the
ground.

Chimpanzees can pick up and hold things with their hands or their feet.

A chimpanzee can hang from a branch by one foot.

In the wild chimpanzees can live for 40 to 50 years. When they are babies, chimpanzees have much to learn about their world.

At a tree full of ripe figs chimpanzees may stay together for a week, eating and having fun.

Most of the time chimpanzees travel around in small groups looking for food.

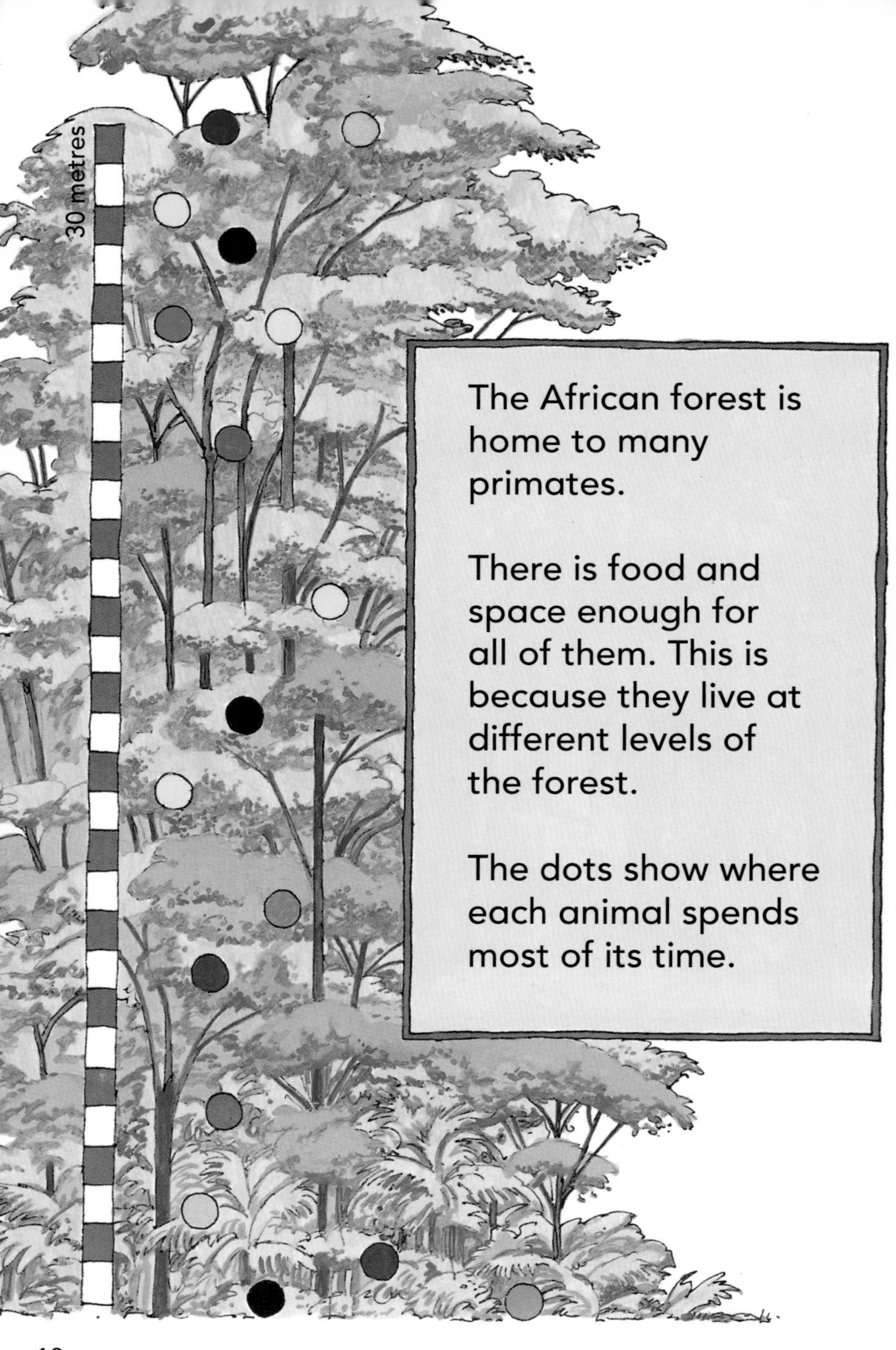

The African forest is home to many primates.

There is food and space enough for all of them. This is because they live at different levels of the forest.

The dots show where each animal spends most of its time.

Chimpanzee
Red colobus monkey
Potto
Angwantibo
Mangabey
Galago
Mona monkey
Bush baby
De Brazza guenon
Gorilla
Mandrill

Chimpanzees are clever.

When they hunt for food, they use tools to help them.

Using a grass stem to collect termites.

Using chewed-up leaves as a sponge to soak up water.

Collecting ants with a stick.

Cracking open a nut with a stone.

Humans, gorillas, chimpanzees, orangutans and bonobos belong to a group of primates called the great apes.

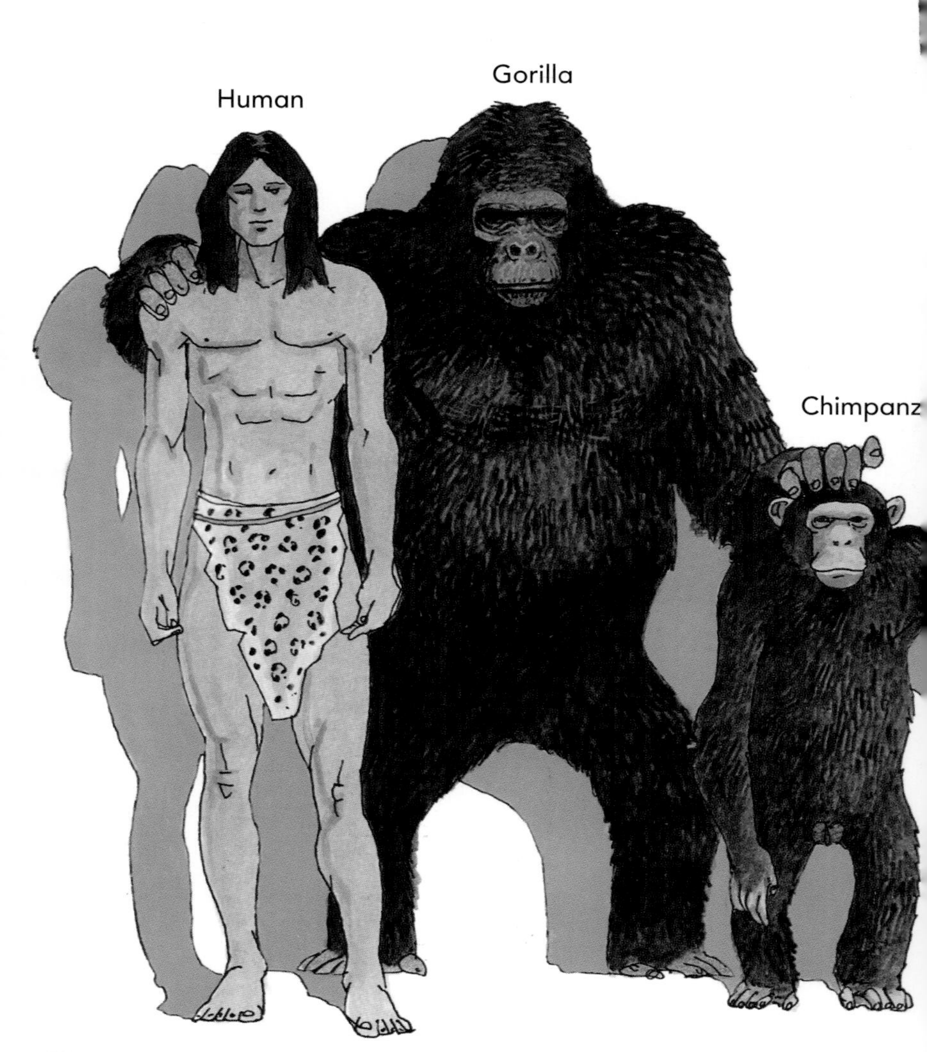

The great apes do not have tails. They are bigger than other primates.

The great apes have large brains.

Humans are interested in other great apes. These animals are like humans in many ways.

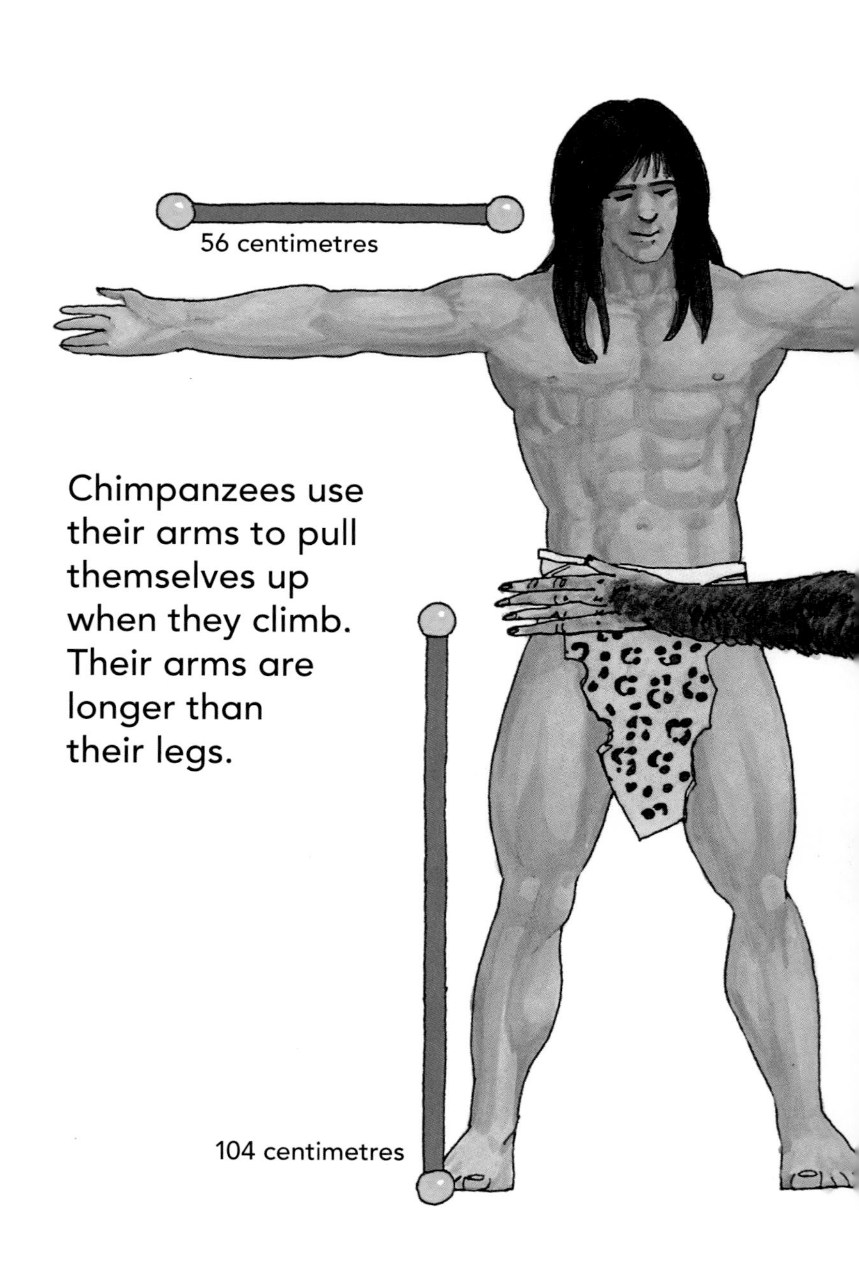

Chimpanzees use their arms to pull themselves up when they climb. Their arms are longer than their legs.

Chimpanzees and humans can judge distances. This helps when they are swinging through trees or crossing the road.

Chimpanzees have powerful teeth and strong jaws for chewing.

A chimpanzee's canine teeth are bigger than a human's. They are good weapons. The side teeth grind up hard nuts and leaves. The incisors cut through fruits.

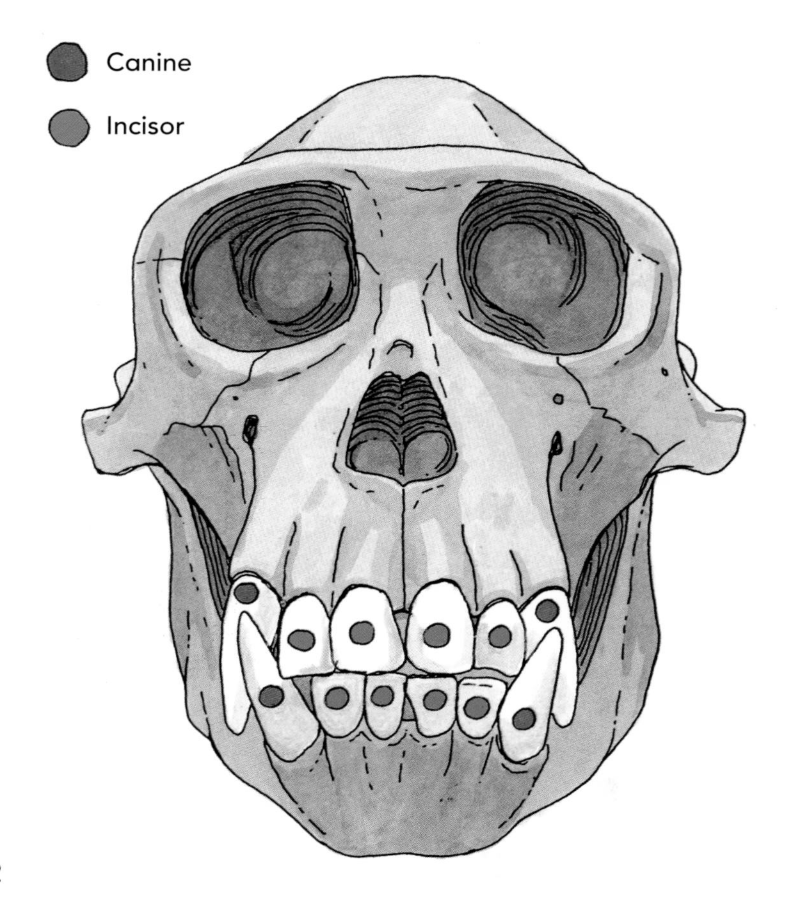

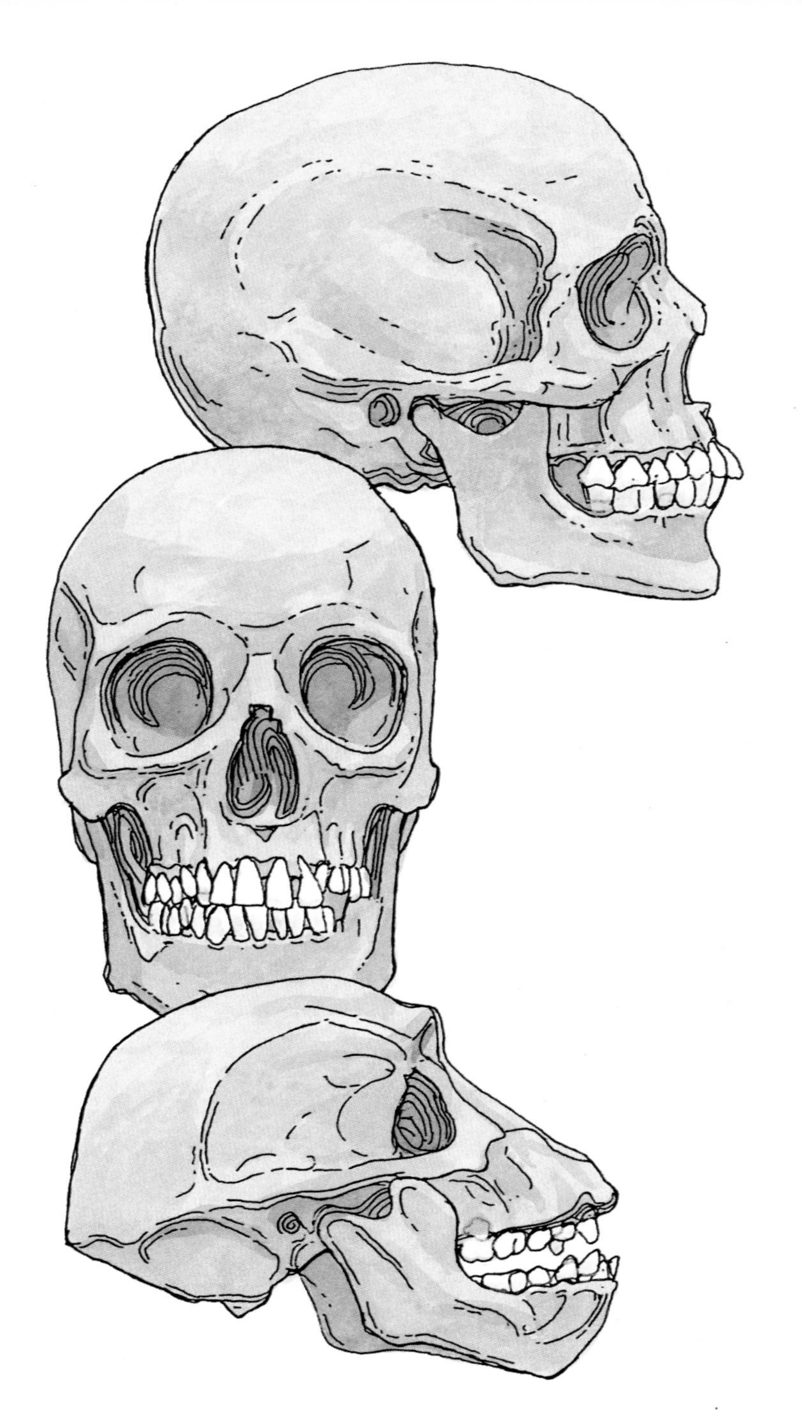

Chimpanzees and monkeys travel through the trees in different ways.

Monkeys walk and run along tree branches on all fours.

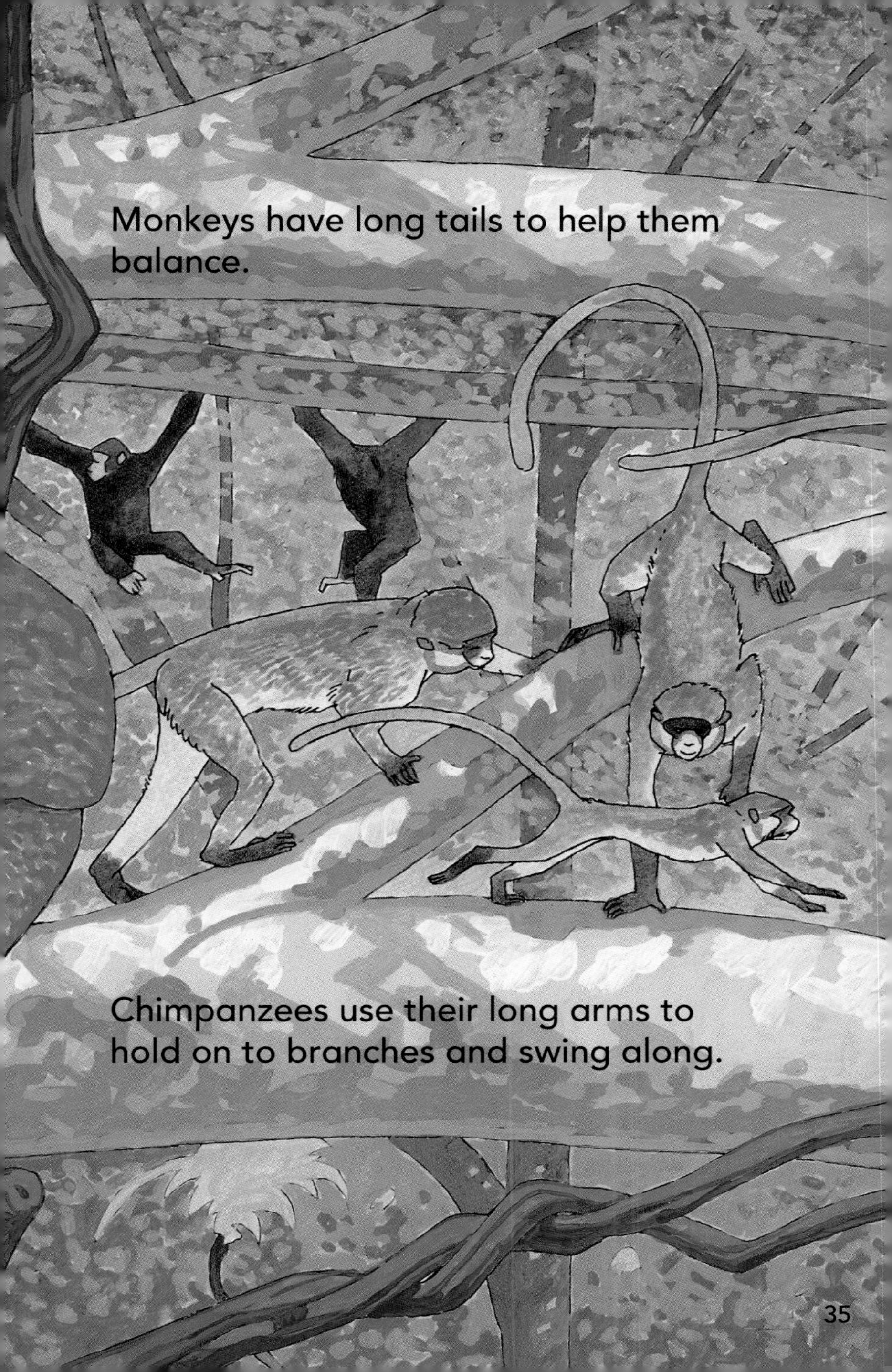

Monkeys have long tails to help them balance.

Chimpanzees use their long arms to hold on to branches and swing along.

Animals that live in cold climates have more than one layer of fur to keep them warm.

Chimpanzees live in a hot climate. They do not need thick fur to keep them warm. They have only one layer of fur or hair. When they grow old, chimpanzees, like humans, can lose their hair.

Groups of chimpanzees live in territories of five to 20 square kilometres. Male chimpanzees will defend the group's territory.

Chimpanzees from other groups are not welcome in another group's territory.

They may be chased and attacked by the males defending their territory.

Male chimpanzees "display" to show how powerful they are. They will stand up, drag and throw branches and rocks and stamp on the ground.

Other males are
scared and go away.
Fights between
males from different
communities can
end with one of the
animals being killed.

Female chimpanzees start breeding at about 13 years.

When a female is ready to mate her bottom swells and turns pink.

Males will often take a female chimpanzee away from the group to mate.

Newborn chimpanzees weigh about 1.8 kilograms. They hold on to the hair on their mother's chest and stomach and go everywhere with her.

At five to six months old the baby chimpanzee starts riding on its mother's back.

If its mother dies, an infant chimpanzee may die of sadness.

Chimpanzees have different personalities. They can be shy, aggressive, playful or kind.

They feel sadness, loneliness, joy, fear and anger.

Happy, at play

Worried

Aggressive

Happy, content

This girl is happy. This chimpanzee is afraid.

Being friends with a chimpanzee can be confusing.

Chimpanzees hold hands, pat each other, and hug and kiss to show friendship. They groom each other, picking out dry skin and dirt.

Grooming is another way chimpanzees show friendship. A chimpanzee grooming a higher ranked member of the group is showing respect.

15
metres

Chimpanzees sleep about nine to 15 metres up in the trees. Every night they make a nest to sleep in. Bending and weaving branches together, they make a bed and line it with grass and leaves. They are safe and warm in their nests.

"Tarzan of the Apes" is a story about a human baby who is left in the jungle. The apes look after him. When he grows up he is the leader of the apes.

Tarzan is strong. He swings through the jungle from tree to tree like a chimpanzee. He protects the jungle animals from hunters.

In 1961 a chimpanzee was put into a spaceship and sent on a 16 minute space flight. It was very frightened. Other chimpanzees were also sent into space.

Because it was safe for chimpanzees
to go into space in a rocket, the first
humans went up soon after.

People who study how chimpanzees live and work together think this must be how early humans lived.

Early humans may have looked more like chimpanzees than humans do now.

Leopards will hunt and kill chimpanzees, but humans are their worst enemy.

Humans hunt them for food and catch them to sell as pets.

Chimpanzees are also taken away to be used in medical research.

The forests where chimpanzees live are being cleared for logging, mining, growing crops, and housing.

Some people are trying to keep safe places for chimpanzees. Others are working to improve the lives of chimpanzees in captivity.

Glossary

alpha male • the lead male in a community.
captivity • being in a cage or other place instead of being free.
community • family group.
elders • older members of a group.
grooming • cleaning and combing the fur of another animal.
mammal • animal whose young is fed on milk from the mother's body.
medical research • work and study to improve people's health and the treatment of illness.
peers • animals of the same age.
predator • animal that hunts and kills other animals for its food.
prey • animal that is hunted and killed by another animal.
primates • group of mammals that includes apes, monkeys and humans.
rump • the hind part of a mammal.
sponge • something that soaks up liquid.
territory • the area of land that an animal hunts in and defends against other animals.
warm-blooded animal • an animal whose blood temperature stays at between 36 and 44 degrees Celsius in cold or hot weather. Humans keep their temperature at this level in winter by wearing warm clothes.

Index

Africa 3, 18, 59
alpha male 14–15
angwantibo 19

baboon 5
bonobo 23
bush baby 19

cat (house) 8
chimpanzee
  appearance 6–7, 11, 24–25, 26, 36–37
  breeding 42–43, 44–45
  communication 1
  communities 13, 14–15, 16, 41
  "display" 40–41
  eyesight 30–31
  food 16–17, 18, 20–21
  grooming 48–49
  in space 54–55
  life span 12–13
  personality 46–47
  predators 58
  size 6–7, 8–9, 10, 24–25
  teeth 32–33
  territories 38–39
  use of tools and weapons 1, 20–21, 40
  where it lives 2–3, 18, 51, 59

De Brazza guenon 5, 19

early humans 56
elders 13
emperor tamarin 4

forest 2, 3, 18, 59

galago 19
gorilla 5, 19, 22
great apes 22–23

house cat 8
humans 1, 4, 22–23, 24–25, 27, 28–29, 30–31, 32
hunters 53, 58

impala 27

Japanese macaque 4

lemur, ring-tailed 5
leopards 58
lion 29

mammals 1
mandrill 19
mangabey 19
medical research 58
mona monkey 19
monkeys 5, 19, 34–35

orangutan 4, 23

potto 19
primates 4, 18, 22–23

red colobus monkey 19
ring-tailed lemur 5

"Tarzan of the Apes"
52–53
termites 20

vervet monkey 5

weapons 1

zebra 26, 28